Legal Disclaimers

This book is presented to you for informational purposes only and is not a substitution for any professional advice. The contents herein are based on the views and opinions of the author and all associated contributors.

While every effort has been made by the author and all associated contributors to present accurate and up to date information within this document, it is apparent technologies rapidly change. Therefore, the author and all associated contributors reserve the right to update the contents and information provided herein as these changes progress. The author and/or all associated contributors take no responsibility for any errors or omissions if such discrepancies exist within this document.

The author and all other contributors accept no responsibility for any consequential actions taken, whether monetary, legal, or otherwise, by any and all readers of the materials provided. It is the readers sole responsibility to seek professional advice before taking any action on their part.

Readers results will vary based on their skill level and individual perception of the contents herein, and thusly no guarantees, monetarily or otherwise, can be made accurately. Therefore, no guarantees are made.

Introduction

Congratulations! You're getting married!

The first thing you should do is run over to SignatureWeddingAisleRunners.com and get yourself a custom aisle runner. I know, shameless plug. The second thing you should do is let your love ones know when the wedding is going to take place.

If you're looking for information on Save The Date Cards, you've come to the right place. Because I have 101 Unique Ideas For Save The Date Cards right here in this guide!

Save The Date Cards are a great way to let your guests know that there's a wedding being planned. And they are especially considerate to send in order notify in advance those guests whom you really want to attend your wedding who will be traveling long distances or may have to make special work arrangements.

Since Save The Date cards have only been in use since the 1990s, there really are no particular rules of etiquette for their use. So you're free to do whatever you like with them. Go ahead! Express yourself! And don't worry about being all prim and proper and formal....unless you really want to, that is. If that's the case, then by all means, order some Save The Date Cards that will match your invitations.

It is suggested that you mail out Save The Date cards at least eight to ten months before your wedding. This gives your guests from far away plenty of time to make arrangements for travel and lodging and to get time off work if necessary. If your wedding is going to be near a holiday or a time of year when travel in your area is particularly heavy, then you'll want to give your guests plenty of notice.

As to WHO you send Save The Date cards to – it's not

necessary to send them to everyone on your guest list. Most of your guests, especially those who won't have to travel very far, will be fine receiving only your invitation. That's assuming, of course, that you plan to send out your invitations at least 4 to 6 weeks in advance.

Be sure to send Save The Dates, as well as your invitations, as early as possible if your wedding will be during a holiday season or if you're planning a destination wedding where everyone will have to go to Mexico or Hawaii, etc.

You only need to send Save The Date Cards to those people who you really want to be at your wedding and who will need the advance notice to make whatever arrangements are necessary to be there. When these people receive your Save The Date card, they're going to know that you really want them at your wedding, and they will make the necessary plans to be there.

So, if you DON'T really want your third cousin twice removed on your second cousins side of the family to attend your wedding, but your mother says you have to invite her anyway, then do NOT send her a save the date card. Just send her invitation at the same time you send all the others and hope for the best!

The only information you need to include on the Save The Date card is your names, and your wedding date and the place, if you know where it's going to be. If not, at least let them know what city so they can start looking at travel arrangements. And include somewhere near the bottom of the card - "Invitation To Follow".

The best thing about Save The Date cards is that you may not have to send many of them, so you can be creative without breaking the bank!

Anytime you can work a magnet onto any of these ideas, it

would be very helpful. You can buy strips of magnets at the craft store and you can just cut it to fit. A magnet will make it easier for your guest to hang onto the "card" because they can stick it on on their refrigerator or filing cabinet. Of course, a magnet won't work for all of these ideas, but, if you can include one, it would be a good idea.

Some of these ideas call for pretty card stock paper and you can find that at your local office supply store. But I'd go to your local craft store first. They have a much better selection and then they also have all these great stickers and really neat embellishments that you use to do scrapbooks. You can find all kinds of unique ideas to add to any of these Save The Dates that you see here.

While you're at the craft store, check the wedding aisle and the seasonal aisle for unique little plastic candy containers and different colored favor boxes. And use your imagination! Any of these ideas can be personalized with ribbons, or sequins or stickers or feathers or flowers or....well, you get the idea.

And some of these ideas might cost a little more than one stamp to mail, too. If you're concerned about expense, I suggest you make up one sample, package it for mailing or shipping, and then take it to the post office to see how much it weighs.

101 Save The Date Ideas

This guide features fun and creative Save The Date Ideas that will hopefully lead you in the right direction while planning your wedding. Whatever you end up creating, just make sure that you have fun and let your personalities shine though!

Luggage Tags

Since most of the people you'll be sending these Save The Date cards to will be traveling from some distance to attend your wedding, send them luggage tags with your Save The Date information tucked inside the pocket. Not only will they remember your wedding, but it will remind them they need to get luggage for the trip! And maybe they'll think about getting you a set of luggage, too, as a wedding gift!

Coconuts Anyone?

2

Getting married in Hawaii? Write you Save The Date information on a coconut and pop it in the mail! Yes! It's legal to mail a coconut, as is, in any state in the Union. No packaging required! You can either write the information directly on the coconut or print goofy labels on your computer.

Message in a Bottle

Save the Date Ideas

3

Ooh! A beach wedding! How about putting a little bit of sand in a bottle, then write your Save The Date information of a nice piece of parchment paper, and into the bottle it goes! Don't forget the cork!

Paper Boats

Or better yet, for that beach wedding, get some pretty pastel colored card stock and make paper boats. You can get card stock or heavy, decorative papers at your local craft shop. And while you're there, check out the scrapbook supplies. You'll be able to find all kinds of beach related stickers and embellishments to decorate your sailboats with.

Photo Strips

5

Photo strips are all the rage right now! Visit one of those photo booths at your mall or at the beach. You usually get 4 picture per sitting. Plan ahead, and in the first picture, you and your fiancé can hold a card that says, "Save The Date". In the second picture, hold another card that has your names written on it. For the third picture, your card will say "Are Getting Married". And then for the fourth picture, hold up a card that says the date. Be sure to make very silly faces for each picture!

Chocolate Bars

6

Send personalized Chocolate Bars! If you're handy with your computer you can get wrapper software and make your own personalized candy bar wrappers. If you're not so creative, check on line for one of the many websites where you can order custom made candy bars and you can choose the wrappers. Better order a few extra!

Scrabble

7

Do you and your fiancé love to play Scrabble? Set up the Scrabble board and spell out your Save The Date information with the tiles. Then take a picture of it and turn it into a postcard.

Order Take Out

8

Send them Chinese Take-Out! You can buy the little cartons the Chinese take-out comes in at the craft store. They usually have decorative containers, too, for the different holidays. Or get plain white containers and decorate with stickers or paints or permanent markers. Then fill them up with some pretty tissue paper. AND THEN – there are loads of websites where you can order customized Fortune Cookies. And you don't need to order a ton of them either. Have them print your Save The Date information on the fortune! You might need to order extra of these, too!

Spirits

9

Some friends of mine recently got married in Jamaica.
Boy, did we have fun! Anyway, they went to the liquor
store and got little mini bottles of Jamaican Rum to use as
a Save The Date. They made little tags on their computer
and tied them onto the necks of the bottles with some
ribbons. Too cute!

Play Ball!

My brother and his wife are huge baseball fans and when they got married they mailed everyone on the Save The Date Announcement a baseball! They went to the sporting goods store and bought brand new, shiny white baseballs and carefully took them out of the packaging so they could hand letter their Save The Date info on them. Then back in the boxes they went and off to the post office!

Keychains

11

Make SURE they don't forget the date and send them a personalized keychain! I mean, they always have their keys, right? You can buy cute little clear plastic key chains at the craft store and they have a space so you can put a picture in them. Take a picture of you and your fiancé and print your Save The Date information on the back. They'll always have your information right at hand! Unless they're like me of course. I found MY keys in the refrigerator last week!

Calendars

12

Now here's an idea – a Calendar! Why didn't I think of that? If your computer has a printing program on it, it's likely there's a calendar. If not, there are free printable calendars online and you could print them on nice card stock or use your computer to come up with your own personal design. Don't forget to circle the date before you mail them out!

CDs

13

Send them a song – Burn a CD of you and your fiancés favorite songs, or put together a cool dance mix or country music. Or how about a mix of great make out music?! Print cool labels on your computer for the CD cases and don't forget to include your Save The Date info! Oooooh! Elvis songs! That would be cool!

Postcards

Here's a really inexpensive easy to do idea – send them touristy postcards from the area where you live or where you're holding the wedding. Some of your guests may have never visited your city and they'll get a kick out of a tacky tourist postcard.

Hot Chocolate

If you're getting married in the winter time, another inexpensive idea is hot chocolate packets. Some of the generic brands come in plain white packets that you could decorate in a million different ways. Again, visit your craft store for wintery stickers and embellishments to decorate the packets, or you could print out a really "cool" label on your computer.

Flip Flops

And this is the BEST idea for a beach wedding – get yourself a permanent marker and write your Save The Date information on the soles of some Flip Flops! I LOVE this idea! You can get flip flops in size small, medium or large. And where I live, you can get really inexpensive flip flops at just about any store in town. Check you local dollar store or even the pharmacies in your area. And they don't weigh much so they're very inexpensive to mail. If you don't want to write on the bottoms, print your Save The Date info on some pretty paper and tie it to the flip flops with some coordinating curling ribbon.

Paper Airplanes

17

For a destination wedding, print your Save The Date information on some pretty paper and send them a paper airplane. Make the airplane as simple or as complex as you want. If you are looking for complex paper airplane designs, pull up your favorite search engine and search for "paper airplane designs".

Coffee Mugs

18

Send them a personalized coffee mug and they'll see your Save The Date every morning. Craft stores have ceramic mugs that you can paint or decorate with permanent markers. Or get the plastic mugs and slip in a picture of you and your fiancé.

Wedding in Mexico

19

Getting married in Mexico? Send them mini maracas and attach a little card with your Save The Date with some colorful ribbon. Or tie your Save The Date Announcements onto a jar of salsa with some colorful ribbons.

Winter Weddings

20

Thank goodness for craft stores – send them miniature mittens with your Save The Date card tucked inside for your winter wedding. Or get little gift boxes, put your Save The Date inside, printed on some pretty parchment paper, and wrap it like a little mini Christmas present.

Halloween Weddings

21

For an inexpensive idea for you Halloween wedding, decorate dime store Halloween masks. Or fill miniature plastic pumpkins with Halloween candy. Look for inexpensive tins or containers of Halloween candy and print a Save The Date label on your computer.

Forth of July

22

Celebrate your differences! Use mini flags representing your states or countries. Or use miniature American flags for a Fourth Of July Wedding. Or miniature pennants from your favorite sports teams!

T-Shirt

23

Print it on a T-Shirt! Design your Save The Date announcement on your own computer and print it out on special iron on T-shirt Transfer paper. For summer weddings, think Tank Tops and for Winter Weddings go for Sweat shirts! Check your office supply or craft store, or find it online.

Boarding Pass

24

Use your computer to print them a boarding pass for your destination wedding. You can use a real boarding as a template or you can find boarding pass templates online to use.

Concert Tickets

25

Let them know your wedding is going to ROCK and order Save The Dates printed on concert tickets. You can use an old concert ticket as a guide or try to find a template online.

Email

26

Absolutely FREE! If you or your fiancé are good with your computer, use your graphics program to create ANY design you want to make your Save The Date cards truly unique. Then, just save the file and email it to your guests. Set the reminder on your email calendar to notify you once a month and send your guests monthly updates on your wedding plans.

Flower Pens

27

Make pretty flower pens. If you know what flowers you're using for your wedding, or even if you don't, tightly wrap standard stick pens with green ribbon and hot glue pretty flower on the end. Print Your Save The Date information on a piece of green paper shaped like a leaf and attach with ribbon.

Nascar

28

For those NASCAR lovers – send a Matchbox car with your info attached. And some of these are light enough that you can attach a magnet. How cute would THAT be on your refrigerator?!

Homemade Bookmarks

29

Print your Save The Date information of pretty card stock, laminate it, and add a tassel for a pretty bookmark. Your guests will appreciate the invite and will also have a unique bookmark to use for reading.

Christmas Weddings

Christmas wedding? Bake some Gingerbread Boys and decorate with Royal icing to make them good and sturdy. Once the icing dries, you can write on it with a permanent marker. Use this for any shape of cookie, Christmas stars, or Easter Bunnies. Some gift shops have unique cookie cutters that are shaped like the state or an animal from that state. For example, where I live, all the shops carry alligator cookie cutters. If you cover the top of the cookie with royal icing, it will hold up better in shipping and last longer, too. Well, maybe not in MY house...

Homemade Postcards

31

Have someone take a picture of you and your fiancé and convert it into postcards. Go as silly or as formal as you want here. Let them see the real you while you're holding up a card with your Save The Date information!

Engagement Magnet

32

Use an engagement picture and make a magnet. You can find magnets at the office supply store that are the size of business cards. Just peel off the paper backing and attach your Save The Date photo.

Extra! Extra!

33

Why not take out an as in the local newspaper. Once the paper publishes the ad you can then ask neighbors for the section of the paper that contains the ad and then send it to your guest list. You can also purchase extra copies of the paper if your guest list is on the large side.

Word Find

34

Make it a little interesting and have your Save The Date information hidden in a word find puzzle. You can find websites online that will allow you to enter words and create a word find puzzle containing those words. Make sure that you include the answer on the back of your puzzle, a reference to the answers on the front of the puzzle and instructions. You wouldn't want people not showing up because they couldn't figure it out.

Video Ransom Note

35

Piece together video clips of different people saying each part of your Save The Date message into sort of a video ransom note. For instance, if your wedding date is July 4th, 3000, you would get a single clip of someone saying the words "save", then "the", then "date", then "July", then "4th", then "3000". Once you get the compilation all finished, you could burn it to DVD or upload the video online and send your guest list the URL.

Mystery Note

36

Send your guest list a single piece of "blank mystery" paper with instructions to keep the paper for a certain amount of time. What they won't know is that the "blank mystery" paper contains a hidden message written in invisible ink. Maybe a week or so later send them another note containing instructions on how to make the invisible in on the "blank mystery" paper appear. I know it seems a bit silly but your guests will probably enjoy it.

Internet Scavenger Hunt

37

This one will take a bit on planning. Set up an Internet scavenger hunt where you send you guest list emails everyday for a certain number of days and each email contains a clue. The clue will tell your guest to go to a particular website and write down something. That could be a letter from the phrase Save The Date and your actual wedding day or it would be a word from the phrase Save The Date and your actual wedding date. You can add your own imagination to this one.

Etch a Sketch

38

Sketch out your Save The Date information on an Etch A Sketch. This might take some practice before your get really good. Even if you don't get good, so what. This is all about fun right? Once you get your design just the way you want it after several attempts, record it! Then you can upload the video online and forward the URL to your guest list. Your video should get PLENTY of views.

If you have the budget, you may be able to hire an artist to do this for you and record his creation. Try searching online for "Etch A Sketch artist" and see what you come up with. Try contacting one of the artist that show up for that search term. You may be able to strike up a deal.

Business Cards

39

You can find many companies today that sell business cards online at a super low price. Well, just replace your Save The Date information where there should be business info and viola, you have got about 500 Save The Date business cards at a relatively low price.

Make Up a Song

Yeah, this sounds completely corny, but your guests will probably get a kick out of it. Make up a song about your wedding. Maybe throw in there how you met and the whole nine yards. Then at the end of the song throw in your Save The Date information. Upload your song the the web and then send this to your guest list.

Multi-Lingual

41

Send your Save The Date information completely in a random language that none of your guests would know. To do this search online for "English to OTHER LANGUAGE translation", where "OTHER LANGUAGE" is whatever language you want to translate your massage to. You will fin many different websites that will do this for you. Once you translate the massage, make sure that you send translated Save The Date message along with where your guests can translate the message back into English.

Morse Code

Here is a military wedding idea. Believe it or not, there are websites out there that can translate words into Morse Code. Search for the term "translate text to morse code" and you should find a decent numbers of websites that do this. Type in your Save The Date information and then translate. Some website will even allow you to download your Save The Date message translated into morse code. You can then burn this to a CD and send it out to your guests. Be sure to include a note telling the guests what the message means, unless of course they would already know what it means.

Legos

43

You and your fiancé and build a Lego chapel, equipped with bride and groom standing at the front. You can write a message with your Save The Date info and place it next to the Lego chapel. You can either record the building of the actual chapel and send that to your guests or simple take a picture of the finished product and send that to your guests.

Directions

44

This one make take a great deal of time and effort. If you do it right though, you may be able to knock it out in a weekend. Find the address of each and every guests and print out directions from their houses to the place where you will be married. The good thing about this is that you will only have to change the starting point each time. Once these directions are printed out, be sure to include the Save The Date Information somewhere on the directions.

Got Kids?

This will work if you have a little one that is just learning how to write. Show your little one how to write your Save The Date message on a piece of the training paper they use to learn how to write. After a couple of tries, take the finished product to be photocopied. There you have it. You have an extremely cheap and SUPER cute Save The Date invitation.

Power Point Presentation

46

You and your fiancé can put together a Power Point presentation for your Save The Date invites. You can include great information such as how you met, the time and location of the wedding and directions. Be sure sure to throw in a few interesting tidbits to keep your guests interested.

Piece By Piece

47

Send your Save The Date information piece by piece to your guests. Of course if your guests list is large then you may not want to do this but if it is reasonable send each guests a piece of the Save The Date one week at a time. Be sure to include instructions on each piece stating that the guest should keep each piece and at the end they can put together the entire message.

Glass Slippers

If you wedding theme is based around being a princess, try sending your guest a glass slipper Save The Date. Search online for the term "toy glass slippers" and you should find websites that sell these. You can create a bunch of notes and slip them into the glass slippers.

Thumb Drives

49

Are you a "techy" or sort of a "geek"? Create a message will all your information on it and load it on a thumb drive. They are light weight and easy to mail. Be sure to include a separate slip of paper with the thumb drive containing the message on the thumb drive, just in case you send it to someone who doesn't have a computer or whose computer can't read thumb drives.

Movie Tickets

50

You can get your info printed on movie tickets. How cool would that be? Search online for the term "custom movie tickets" and you should find plenty of companies that will print whatever you want on movie tickets for you. Put in the note that you send you guests that the movie tickets are required for admission into the wedding.

Sunscreen

51

If you're planning a beach wedding, send your Save The Dates a bottle of sunscreen. Either create a custom label for the bottle or ties on a pretty Save The Date card that you've printed on your computer.

Spring Flower Seeds

52

Getting married in the summer?   Print your Save The Date information on packets of Spring Flower Seeds. As the flowers start blooming it will remind your guests they need to be making their plans.

Ornaments

53

For a Christmas wedding, personalize an ornament. You can use regular ornaments from the Christmas aisle or visit your local craft shop for ceramic, glass, plastic or wooden ornaments that you can totally customize. Use mini silk flowers, ribbon, sequins, paint, glitter... you'll have a hard time deciding WHAT you want to do with these when you see all the possibilities at the craft store!

Easter Weddings

54

If your wedding is near Easter, send them a mini Easter Basket! You can buy mini baskets at craft stores and include a few pastel Jordan Almonds. Jelly beans are available year round, too. Add a little colorful paper filler and tie it up in a pretty piece of tulle with a nice bow and your Save The Date information.

To make it even easier, put a few jelly beans into one of those plastic Easter eggs and include your Save The Date information.

Christmas Beach Weddings

~55~

Let your Save The Date guests know you're having a
Christmas Beach Wedding...somewhere warm, I hope!
You can buy clear plastic Christmas tree ornaments that
open up like those plastic Easter eggs you had as a kid.
Fill them with a little sand and a few seashells....and your
Save The Date information, of course! This looks cute in
antique bottles, too, for a Vintage summer wedding.

Lifesavers

You can't live without him! Let everybody know he's your lifesaver by personalizing...a roll of Lifesavers! Carefully remove the outer wrap from a roll of Lifesavers and use it as a template to design your own label. Use your computer to design a cool graphic or check out the different rubber stamps at the craft store. Or order custom Lifesaver wrappers online.

Personalized Pens

57

Order personalized pens from any one of a number of online printers or your local office supply store. These are inexpensive enough and cheap enough to mail, that you could send them to everyone on your guest list. Heck, order a bunch and use them for wedding favors.

Flip Book

58

Here is another idea that you will probably need to video tape. Make a flip book containing your Save The Date information. It can also contain other info that you would like the guests to know. When it is completed, take a video of you flipping though the book and posts the completed video online for all your guests to view.

Cross Word Puzzle

Create a unique crossword puzzle for your guests to figure out. Each clue can be related to a different word in your Save The Date message. For the clue for the word "save" could be - "The opposite of delete". Another example for the word "date" would be - "A dark reddish brown fruit, oval, and about 1 1/2 inches long". Okay, that last clue was a stretch but you get the idea.

Go Green

60

Use reusable green shopping bags as your Save The Dates. You can buy a bunch of these for your guests and customize them. Each and every time they go to the grocery store they will be reminded of your wedding.

Telegrams

61

This may only work if you have a minimal guest list or if you have a big enough budget to do so. Hire a telegram service to personalized each message with your wedding date information in it. This may be a bit expensive but your wedding guest will surely get a kick out of it.

All In

62

Print your wedding date information on poker chips. There are many companies out there that will allow you to print a message on a poker chip. Some of the messages are done with labels which would be much more cost effective and others actually hot print the message right on the poker chip itself. You can choose which type you would like depending on how big or small your budget is.

Flashlights

63

Include your Save The Date information inside of a flashlight. You can also include a note saying that you are marrying the "light of your life". Yeah, it's kind of corny but it is also cute too.

Caricatures

Find an artist to do caricatures of you and your fiancé. Make sure the artist injects a little bit of humor and your individual personalities into the pictures. You can then use these pictures as your Save The Dates. Search online for "caricature artist" and you should be able to find plenty of artists to choose from.

Wedding Jokes

65

You and your fiancé can make up a bunch of wedding jokes and include them with your Save The Dates. If you don't know many wedding jokes you can find many of them online. Search for the term "corny wedding jokes" and there will be plenty of websites to choose from.

Florida Weddings

66

Getting married in Florida? Send them a Pink Flamingo Refrigerator Magnet. And if it's a Christmas wedding, make sure it's got a little Santa cap on! Or an alligator magnet, or a surf board magnet, or a fish magnet, or a boat magnet....you get the picture!

Christmas Save The Dates

67

There are sooo many ideas for Christmas Save The Dates
-

Fill Miniature Stockings with a Candy Cane and your Save
The Date

Send everyone a pair of warm mittens

Make little bags of Mulled Cider spices and tie with pretty
ribbon and a cinnamon stick

Personalized Decorated Sugar Cookies

Tie 3 or 4 Candy Canes in a pretty bundle with fancy
ribbons

Recipes

68

If you enjoy spending time in the kitchen, send them your Recipe For Love - and include your Save The Date information – on a recipe card. If you don't like the Recipe For Love idea, just send a recipe for the particular season in which you are getting married.

Oven Mitts

69

If your guests know you as an expert cook than you can tuck your Save The Date information in an oven mitt. You may be able to find a wholesaler that sells these sorts of items wholesale online so that you can save a few bucks.

Soap

Are you crafty? Because I have a really neat idea and it's really very easy. Make everybody a bar of soap and include little wedding type charms inside of it so as the soap is used the little charms will appear!

The pour, mold Soap, molds, fragrances, colors and even essential oils can be found online.

Seashell Molds for a beach wedding

Rubber Duck molds for Spring weddings

Heart Molds for Romantic weddings

Loaf Molds for any occasion

Star Molds for Christmas or 4th of July weddings

Frog Molds – tell them you finally found your prince!

Soap (continued)

When making the Melt And Pour type of soaps you really just need a few pieces of equipment. Follow the manufacturers suggestions for melting, but, basically all you do is melt down the bulk soap, stir in your color and fragrance, and then pour it into a mold. Melting can be done in the microwave or a double boiler and only takes a few minutes.

Let the soap set for a few minutes I the molds then tuck in your charms. It only takes a few hours for the soap to be set all the way. And even the clean up is easy – it's soap!

Care Packages

76

For a really thoughtful Save The Date idea visit hotels and motels in your area and get their business cards and brochures and put together a little "Care" package for your out of towners. Include a map if they'll be driving, or directions from the airport. Include a touristy "Wish You Were Here" post card and a bunch of those tourism pamphlets you always find in hotel lobbies. And if you can get one or two of the hotels to give you some of their mints with their logos on them, those would be fun to throw in the package, too.

Sunglasses

77

When you think summer – think sunglasses! And the wilder the better! Find silly sunglasses at souvenir shops and either tie on a Save The Date Card or make a sticker to put on the lenses. If you do the stickers, though, make sure they're the kind that will easily peel off. Even though they're goofy sunglasses, someone may still want to wear them.

Photo CD

78

Show them who you REALLY are! If some of these far away guests haven't seen you for years, and if they've never even met your fiancé, put some of your photos on a CD, set it to music, and throw in some funny slides and images. Make up CD covers or labels with your computer that show your Save The Date information. Oh, and don't forget to include baby pictures.

Stamps

Remind them every time they pay their bills! I don't know if THAT'S such a good idea or not – but....order everybody a roll of stamps. You can get custom postage stamps now so use a picture of you and your fiancé, holding an envelope with the date clearly written on it.

Miniature Cauldrons

80

If your wedding is near Halloween, fill miniature cauldrons with a few pieces of Halloween candy and your Save The Date information. Or paint silly faces on miniature pumpkins. Or BUY miniature pumpkins with the faces already painted on at your grocery store in the produce department.

Toiletry Bags

81

For another thoughtful idea, fill up inexpensive toiletry bags that you pick up at the dime store with travel size tooth-paste, shampoo, soap, etc.

Novel + Bookmark

If you know they're going to have a long flight or auto trip, send them a favorite romance novel or a puzzle book with your Save The Date Information printed on a Bookmark. Tell them "'We're sending you this so you have something to keep you occupied on your long trip to be here for our wedding." Or burn a CD with some Road Trip Tunes on it.

New Year's Eve Weddings

For a New Year's Eve wedding, decorate inexpensive paper masks with feather and lots of gold and silver ribbons and sequins. Put your Save The Date information and a magnet on the back! Or put a magnet on a noise-maker or miniature champagne glasses that you can find at the craft store..

Police or Sheriff Badges

Make magnets out of little plastic Police or Sheriff badges and tell them you finally caught your man! You can also include some plastic handcuffs or something of that nature.

Wedding Blogs

85

One of the very best Save The Date Ideas you can do for ALL your guests is to set up your own Wedding Blog. You can use the blog to keep your guests updated on all your wedding plans, the church, the time, the reception hall, the colors, even let them know where you're registered and the items you've put on your list.

If you've never blogged before there are lots of free blogging resources available specifically for the brides. They're free and you don't have to worry about hosting.

Just send the address on to all of your guests and let them know about your blog so they'll be sure to check it regularly. You could even send them an email every time you add something new to the blog to remind them to stop by for a visit.

Wedding Blogs (continued)

85

BUT – if you're an experienced blogger, then you already know the monetary benefits of a blog, the earning potential. Why not set up your own wedding blog, on your own hosting, and monetize it with some of these affiliate items that YOU'RE buying? Who knows better what to sell a bride than a bride who's currently planning her own wedding?

At the very least, you could set yourself up an Amazon wedding blog, put up a Wish List Widget for wedding gifts, and let your friends and family use YOUR blog to do their Amazon shopping. Not only do you get the gifts, you get the commission off of those gift sales from Amazon.

Magazine Subscription

86

If you've got the time, and just a few people that you need to send Save The Dates too, why not sign them up for a monthly magazine subscription? You can usually get the first couple of months free. And they'll be reminded of your wedding every month when the next issue arrives. You could even send a different magazine to each person, one that reflects their own interests. Or send the a bridal magazine to really jog their memories.

Pinwheels

87

Buy cheap pinwheels at the dime store, or make them
yourself with some pretty papers or card stock and write
your Save The Date Information on each "Petal".

New York Weddings

88

Getting married in New York? Surely there are plenty of Statue Of Liberty souvenirs out there that could be made into magnets. Or paint her dress in the colors of your wedding, add some ribbons and bows and attach your Save The Date Announcement.

Traditional

89

If you'd like a more traditional look, office supply stores and craft shops all carry some beautiful stationery that will work in your printer. Get letter size and type up a nice letter to everyone with all of the pertinent information, and include names of hotels and rental car companies in your area.

Paper Cubes

90

Plain white note paper cubes work really well for a Save The Date Announcements! Think about it. That cube will be sitting right there on their desk, right by the calendar. They'll see it every time they sit down. And you can decorate the cubes any way you want!

Traditional Magnets

Save The Date Magnets are really one of the most popular options for Save The Date announcements because they can be placed on the refrigerator and everyone sees them all the time. And your options for ordering are only limited by your own imagination. Most of the magnets can be customized with your own photo so you can make them serious, romantic, whimsical, thoughtful, whatever mood or theme you want to express.

Seattle Weddings

92

Wedding in Seattle? Or are you all coffee lovers? Send individual packets of gourmet coffees. Find them at the grocery store or stop by Starbucks on your way home from work and pick up a variety of flavors.

Miniatures

93

Miniatures! Miniature ANYTHING! Send mini jars of jelly, mini liquor bottles, mini vases, mini bottles of sand, mini bottles of perfume, anything miniature! Tie your Save The Date card on with pretty ribbon or make elegant labels with your computer that contain all the pertinent information. And stick a magnet on the back whenever possible!

Winter Tropical Weddings

94

Wedding on a tropical island in the winter? Check craft shops for miniature glass bottles with cork stoppers. Then throw in a few pieces of charcoal like you use for a fish aquarium, and maybe a sliver of an orange crayon and send them a Hawaiian Snowman, or a Florida Snowman, or a Tahitian Snowman. Put a magnet on the back and don't forget to attach your Save The Date information.

Wine or Beer

95

Send bottles of wine or micro brewed beers that are made in your area. Or pick up the sale wine at the grocer store and make your own labels.

Matching Save The Dates

96

If you've already ordered your invitations, don't forget to see if they have Save The Date Cards available that coordinate with your invitations. Not everyone wants to be wild and kooky. Perhaps you'd like to be a little more formal or traditional.

As a side note, SignatureWeddingAisleRunners.com can recreate the design used on your invitations and Save The Dates on a custom aisle runner and/or table runner. This will really carry your theme/design throughout your wedding day.

Vintage Weddings

97

For a Vintage Wedding, shop your local antique stores and flea markets for pretty lace handkerchiefs that are in good condition and not stained. Have your local seamstress use her embroidery machine to put your Save The Date information in the corner. Or look for pretty costume jewelry that you could turn into magnets, or antique bottles that you could use for "Message In A Bottle" announcements.

Glamor Weddings

98

For a Glamor wedding, look for elegant little pill boxes at gift shops, or even your local pharmacy. Pretty compacts are nice, too. Or a silver-tone or gold-tone lipstick case. Check antique shops, too. Then print your Save The Date information on a nice piece of parchment and roll it into a scroll and tie with very small ribbon.

Flower Power!

99

If you're more the flower child type, make miniature bouquets with very tiny straw flowers. Either tie them up with a pretty ribbon or insert into miniature glass bottles and add on your Save The Date Announcement. Don't forget the magnet!

Disposable Cameras

100

Everyone wants wedding pictures! And everyone loves to take them! Send everybody a disposable camera and tell them No Camera – No Admittance! Find inexpensive flip photo albums at the dime store and fill them part way with pictures of you and your fiancé. Then, include your Save The Date Announcement at the end and let them know there will be plenty more pictures to finish filling their album.

Imagination

101

Idea #101 is simply to use your imagination. You don't want to spend a whole lot of time or money on this because you have so many more important things you need to be taking care of. But it is important to take care of this as soon as possible. If you really want that person who lives on the other side of the planet to be at your wedding, you have to give them plenty of notice.

These Save The Date ideas, or any idea of your own, can be taken care of in one afternoon. Go into any store, a department store, a pharmacy, a dime store, the craft store, the stationery shop, the sporting goods store, the whole foods store, the office supply store....

Go down any aisle, the wedding aisle, the holiday aisle, the toy aisle, the kitchen aisle, the stationery aisle, the school supply aisle....

And use your imagination! Find something that says "YOU" or something that expresses romance or love, or something that says something about the place you're holding the wedding....

Imagination (continued)

101

Just about anything you pick up in any aisle of any store, if it attracted your attention, can be used as a reminder to jog your guests' memories.

Tell yourself you're going into one store and you're only going to spend one hour shopping and when you come out, you're going to have everything you need to send a unique Save The Date Announcement to your guests.

Then, go home, print up the cards if you need to, put everything together and have it done with.

But don't spend any more time searching online or searching through magazines or calling your girlfriends. There are tons of ideas right here in this guide. Either use them as they are, or personalize them for your own use. But don't make a chore of this. This part, the Save The Date Announcements, is supposed to be fun. You have no rules here. So, go ahead! Run with those scissors!

CPSIA information can be obtained at www.ICGtesting.com
Printed in the USA
BVOW03s2239201014

371639BV00027B/456/P